Days of Shame & Failure

Jennifer L. Knox

Days of Shame & Failure
© 2015 Jennifer L. Knox
19 18 17 16 15   1 2 3 4 5

Design & composition: Shanna Compton, shannacompton.com
Cover painting: Charles Browning, "Days of Shame and Failure," © 2015
www.foundrysite.com/browning

Published by Bloof Books
www.bloofbooks.com
New Jersey

Bloof Books are printed in the USA by Bookmobile. Booksellers, libraries, and other institutions may order direct from us by contacting sales@ bloofbooks.com. POD copies are distributed via Ingram, Baker & Taylor, and other wholesalers. Individuals may purchase our books direct from our website, from online retailers such as Amazon.com, or request them from their favorite bookstores.

Please support your local independent bookseller whenever possible.

ISBN-13: 978-0-9965868-0-1
ISBN-10: 0-9965868-1-4
1. American poetry—21st century. 2. Poets, American—21st century.

⊗ This paper meets the requirements of ANSI/NISO Z39.48-1992
(Permanence of Paper).

Big hat, no cattle,
big head, no brain,
big snake, no rattle,
I forever remain.

—Randy Newman

One

Two

Three

One

The New *Let's Make a Deal*

The bedazzled tribe of yahoos has returned
with a new too-tanned, top-heavy prize bunny
swishing her porny French manicure 'round a Frigidaire.
Monty's boorish plaid: swapped for Wayne Brady,
dapper in gray. A woman dressed like a bumblebee,
penciled brows arched in permashock, weighs her options:
a bright pink bow-tied box, or the unknown thing
behind curtain #3. She squints into the din of hoots,
wrings her hands. Life could be made easy in an instant.
"I pick the curtain." Attagirl. The box was a gag: a ham
with straps attached to it. A ham bag. Get it?
Wayne takes a bite to prove the meat's really real
and the audience goes totes bonkers . . . we're interrupted
by news of the hurricane. U.N. delegates have gone on
hunger strike until "a meaningful outcome" is reached.
God, give us one hundred more years until the dawn
of the Kingdom of Roaches, until the sea reclaims Death Valley,
until the end. *Hey, what kind of poem is this?* Behind curtain #3:
a combo washer-dryer bright as a mirrored iceberg.
Bee lady does a shrieking pogo while a guy in a dinosaur
costume mouths, "I love you, Mom!" into the camera.
It's that kind of poem: a poem for the end of the world.

Iowa Plates

Whoever tied the Mylar birthday balloon to the dead squirrel on Main Street thinks big. Cyborg City big. Raisin eyes pressed deep into butter-cookie faces. They don't know how to dance, or snatch. They do know how to run the mouthy object of desire over with a big white truck. Ghost truck. Everywhere, the same truck circling. Dead is nice and quiet. Just the way they like it. A sky-high pile of decapitated dandelions. A chemical moat around the rows. Mushrooms under the elms: hunted, buttered, and gulped down by the pound.

The Comeback

"I thought George Jones was dead," I said, squinting at the singer on stage.

"That's not George Jones. It's *Deinocheirus mirificus*. Archaeologists recently found him in the Gobi desert. I heard about it on NPR," Stan said.

We listened, sipped our beers.

"Did NPR mention how he sounds just like George Jones?"

"No, but maybe he didn't sing in front of them."

The music swelled, and the giant ostrich-dinosaur thing crooned, "It's been a good year for the boh-zoooohs . . ."

Bozos?

"Get off the stage, you goofy-lookin' son of a bitch!" a redneck whooped and whipped a beer bottle at the stage that sailed right past the dinosaur's head, but the goofy-lookin' son of a bitch didn't even flinch.

"How long was he out in that desert?" I asked.

"A kajillion years," Stan said.

"Did NPR say what he'd been doing all that time?"

"Training for a comeback," Stan said.

"Time enough at last," I said, quoting the title of that *Twilight Zone* episode with Burgess Meredith.

"Funny thing about Burgess Meredith . . ." Stan began, his telepathy was soaring in these end times, "you know he was a redhead?"

"I had no idea!" I said.

"You never knew he was a redhead because all the movies he was in were black and white. Then they invented color, but by that time—"

"His hair had gone white!" I interrupted because I knew exactly where we were headed.

The New *Twilight Zone*: "Empty City"

The cloud cover enveloping our hull
splits, shifts to our back like a parachute,
and we descend to the city below.
Its three mighty rivers: now kinked, dribbling
hoses. The scent of seething biomass—
brown mounds going green again with psyched,
thriving mold—reaches as far up as we are—and look:
plumes of smoke snaking into the air there, and there.
Flames and dry backyard blowup pools below coming
into focus, but too much sun to see the windows
in the buildings all have Xs in their eyes.
Between white lines *dash-dash-dashing* the roads:
not a car. The voice on the tower mic:
silent as a pinned moth under glass.

I Cast the Shadow of a Sword over Sky & Sea

Police found a sixty-nine-year-old volunteer clown sodomizing a rare Siberian tiger in an earthquake-ravaged apartment. Precinct reports showed that neighbors had complained of odd smells, sounds, lights, music, and colors coming from the man's house since the Civil War. Along with the tiger, seventy albino bearded dragons were found under the man's waterbed, and a pterodactyl. All of the animals were wearing too much lipstick and prosthetic Hubba Hubba Heinies. In the living room, radioactive waste had leaked through its metal containment barrel and burned a hole through all sixteen floors of the building, straight through to the center of the earth and out the other side. In his statement to the press, the clown denied any wrongdoing: "I are a peaceful man. We be conducting a full investigation into this matter. We half the utmost respect for animals—for lactating women—for Italian-Americans—for the mentally challenged—for the dead." In lieu of an official statement, his wife preferred to let a Bundt cake do the talking.

The Ten-Million-Year War

We'd taken the hill at last! Our muskets flashed
and set our sleeves ablaze! Luminous mercury puddles
purged in our latrine could be seen from outer space
and would eternally endure! Praise His jerky!
"Load the powder muzzle! Hoist the mizzenmast!"
Enemies staggering at us exploded in hollow pops
and rained back down upon us in a gory confetti!
"Know what I could go for?" Bart asked suddenly,
his dank, black mouth full of clouds, and in the hours
of dumbstruck silence that followed, all the dogs
we'd skinned came gallumping happily back to us
with orange croquet balls in their mouths. *Ah-aw.*
"No," I said and meant it. "Tater tots," Bart grinned.
"Tay-der-tots! Tay-der-tots!" we tolled like bells
and toddled around the hill until we all . . . finally . . .
lay down. "Jus' restin' our eyes uhlittlebit."

Indian Head

It occurs to me these throbbing satellite photos
are all we're ever going to get. No formal
announcement from a president or king because
panic: people throwing themselves and their babies
off bridges, running each other over with cars,
spraying bullets into crowds. Why mail out invitations?
Leave a glimmer, a bridge, an *Arbeit Macht Frei*.
We'll go out our most awful regardless. Well,
some will and some will be enough to make the end
berserko. Suits on the news and radio voices will
sputter, then *poof*—nothing more not to say.

I Want to Speak with the Manager

"Promise me" is telling, not asking.

If someone tells you, "Promise me X," you'll probably promise them X and that will probably be a lie because you didn't offer them X.

You were snared.

You were ordered to promise, which means the asker never thought you would do whatever it was of your own free will.

So in a way, you're already off the hook.

Promises are no longer made to me because I'm a middle-aged person.

People stop bothering to lie to you once you've been lied to as many times as I have.

They think you're used to it.

I'm not, and that's a sign of immaturity.

I never tell someone, "Promise me," because nothing's worse than hearing, "I can't promise you that," even though it's always the truth.

I can't handle the truth, apparently.

But surprises do spring up, moments you can force the universe to keep its promises: lifetime warranties, two-for-one Tunnel of Fudge cookies, all-you- can-eat summer Shrimpfest.

Make enough noise, and the universe will give you whatever you want then.

Anything to get rid of you.

Life's Work

At thirteen, Robert Stroud ran away from home and got a job working for the railroad in Alaska where he became a pimp. At eighteen, he murdered a bartender and was sentenced to twelve years on McNeil Island where he stabbed a guard to death and was sentenced to life in solitary confinement at Leavenworth. One morning in the yard, he found a nest with three injured sparrows. He nursed them to health and freed them through the bars on his window. He began ordering canaries through the mail—this was back when prisoners could have pets. Some canaries he kept, the rest he sold to his fellow inmates—men he knew only by their voices—who kept the birds in cages in their cells. Cages within cages. Suddenly, all the canaries began to die. Stroud ordered some books from the library and learned the canaries were suffering from septic fever, an avian plague. He ordered a microscope, discovered a cure, and wrote a book, *Diseases of Canaries*, which has been considered one of the most authoritative books ever written on avian pathology since its publication in 1933, the year my aunt Marilyn was born.

They're buried in the same cemetery in Metropolis, Illinois. Though the cemetery's small, we've never been able to find Stroud's grave. I imagine birds carved into a tall headstone, but since he spent his life in prison, he probably doesn't have a headstone. Or, because he's famous, someone stole it.

Marilyn was fascinated by animals, too—especially cats. She walked the back alleys of that tiny town feeding and tending the strays. There was always something off about her mind, though. Agitated, prone to rage—bipolar. I'm the same way.

Stroud was diagnosed as a psychopath. If the doctors were right, he couldn't have been an animal lover. Psychopaths are incapable of loving anything. Is it possible he did all that work out of boredom?

(For some reason, it strikes me here that the only difference between people is money.)

Stroud was sent to Alcatraz when the guards learned he was making booze from the rubbing alcohol in his lab. Marilyn was kicked out of Bob Jones University for making hard cider in her dorm room closet.

At the end of it, when the voices of people disturbed her—their questions—"Do you want this? Do you want that?"—we would wheel her bed out to the courtyard and leave her awhile under the trees full of birds.

Nature Is Changing Me

against my will.   I believed I was
the train brake, the electric fence,
and that the road unfurled before me
like a ribbon, and the loving car steered
itself for me. I believed my blinks made
shit blow up, my tears made the dog sad,
my tears made the dog sadder than other
people's tears.
                      What I forgot was forgotten
in all dimensions. Erased. What I forgot—
not even a hole or black blasted outline of it
remained. It surprised people—to be so
entirely forgotten. (Take that.) And so it
              surprised me to see that nature is
              forgetting me, and as it does, it is
              changing me into prey that mumbles,
"Bless the heater while it lasts, the apples,
the mushrooms . . .," a thing that goes around
blessing things, playing it safe in the grass.

Between Menus

When the waitress finally toddled back to our table, she looked super weird: all the hard edges of her features (and believe me, they could've cut glass) had melted down in the time that she'd been gone, like a candle—and she wasn't bending her knees when she walked, but was she ever smiling. *Brrr.* She set down some more beers. "How's everything over here?" she asked without moving her lips. "We ordered an hour ago and all you've done is bring us beers we never asked for." Suddenly my ears were flooded with the sound of bees, and I understood, without being told, that some nebulous troubles plagued the kitchen, troubles that I, a corporate lawyer who had never worked in the service industry, couldn't possibly understand. I felt ashamed, but not enough to change my order. "Am I being stubborn or vindictive?" I asked the bees. They didn't answer my question, but revealed inside my eyes a million more words for what I was being.

Poetry Reading at the Fried Chicken & Waffle Hut

The writers get zipped to the gigs on golf carts
like white blood cells to a wound.
But who among us asks the hair-lipped immigrant
slopping up spilt beer with a unwringable mop,
"Where does it hurt—you, of no name tag?"

Syrup overflows the waffle levies. Voices
at the mic are dry, shiny inner tubes.
Lithe arms in the sex poems cast
swan-neck shadows on the bedroom walls.
Friends with beards, picnics, white café lights.
Tits are swell and come in twos.

Only the Beginnings

                                    of books ever held
my attention: the new names stumbling through
their new spaces, the speech between the names,
which is different than the speech inside their heads,
the lies they tell themselves. Give me that anything-
could-happen time—the self-possession, the dignity
before a story takes hold and the author
flogs the characters like slobbery oxen.
                                    In ballet class,
swimming class, Brownies, I drove the teachers nuts
zoning out. Lost in thought—in possibilities—my mouth
hanging open until suddenly some woman was screaming
at me. This happened a lot. But wasn't it my time, too?
Rather, wasn't it *our* time, Mr. Hand?
I'm pretty sure this is why I'm a poet.
                                    The doctor said
Lasik would help me read for longer periods.
But would it make the ends of stories more compelling?
Was that fog in my brain or my eyes, which were getting so
bad, I couldn't proof my work much less read for pleasure?
Alarming discrepancies between what I was seeing and
what was actually there. My therapist said the brain fills in
missing letters on an alphabet line. The brain does the same
with people, I joked—the ex who was all *Q*s and *U*s—
and I'd imagined the rest. "You have to slow down to see
what's really there," he said. Boh-ring. I changed the subject.
I was too impatient, going blind, or both. Who's bored
by resolution? by perfection? by closure?

That's weird, right?

        During Lasik surgery, you can smell your
cornea burning—golden sparks and rainbow laser arcs
shoot off into a furry black ring. How do we keep our
eyes open for this? The next day, I could see the leaves
in Prospect Park blocks away and that's where my vision
has stayed. Three years later, even with glasses, I can't read
long enough to finish a chapter, can't spot where I've
dropped a *the*. It's going to get worse. I should be
more worried, but

        I can't see that far ahead.

Ballet on the Radio

Critics agreed: the solar system redefined minimalism.
It looked best in just a simple blanket *sans* sash.
Like the time we filled the wheelbarrow with feathers,
dumped them, filled it with peanuts, dumped again, etc.
We made do all the way to Sand Mountain like that
without a shovel. Sometimes you got to swing with a
shovel-shaped thing. Swing with he who brung you.
Swing with he who swung you. Sing with splinters
in your tongue—more thought than thorn as thoughts
have hero endings if you're doing it right. You're doing
your best to sync with this ballet on the radio, to sew
a steeple from the static, to turn your scraps into scrap-
books, into book-books, into bookworms, into worms
in the wardrobe made of wet, green wood.

I Led the Horse to Water

because it said it was really thirsty. "Water's
right there—go for it, horsey," I said. "I'm not
gonna drink from that puddle of bilge," it said
disgustedly, then again, "but I'm really, really
thirsty." I looked around. The nearest thing
I could see that wasn't a bush or a mountain
was a gas station, maybe ten miles away
through a curtain of the wavy heat lines coming
off the desert. I could probably get there and
back before the meaner, wilder animals came out
from under their rocks to howl and hunt. I explained
what I had in mind, expecting a whinny or nuzzle
in gratitude. It was a really long walk—I could
die! "I wasn't talking to you—" said the horse staring
off in the other direction, "—I was talking to no one,
to myself maybe, to the mysterious force that led
me here." "Uh, I led you here, you idiot. This is
my puddle," I gestured to the little wooden sign
that read JEN'S PUDDLE in crudely carved letters,
"and you could at least thank me, you big jerk!"
The horse gestured to a littler sign next to it
that read DO NOT DRINK. POISON. He raised
his eyebrows and waited. "Well . . ." I whined,
"you get me all nervous!"

Date Night in Story City

"Do you got car bombs?" the young man asks the waitress.
"Just water," his girlfriend mutters, eyes bolted to the TV.
She's still in scrubs. A nurse? No, too young. Nursing home
aide, maybe—an exhausting gig. She was up before dawn,
I can tell: her bare face, white as a moon. Dyed red hair:
straw straight, air dried. He's dirty like he just got off a farm job,
but his shoes are flashy—too much so and scuffed. Tattoos:
thick, black and blurred like an old sailor's but he can't be
over twenty-four. She's too straight edge for him. He wants
a nice girl. He wants to be a good man. He asks her questions.
Her single-word replies all mean no. So he bobs his head in
time to the music on TV, where she is. We're at the next
table over. "Do you ever get angry like I do?" I ask you.
"You get pretty angry," you say. "I'm sorry about last night."
"Let's just move on," you say and I think it's possible because
you do. The young man beams when the waitress returns:
a glass of water glowing with ice for the girl, and a plastic cup
sloshing whiskey for him—a plastic shot glass with darker
liquid buried in its center like a chrysalis. Plastic, I think,
because drunk people drop the glasses. He cradles it
in both hands (his birthday?) and touches it to her
unmanned glass: a toast to them if she were here.

Settled in the Valley of Descent

When the mist lifts, we see the wild horses grazing.
Like everything here—even wheat—they're a prehistoric breed:
copperplated orange knights. All the hawks.
"What's that?" I ask, peering through a wavy pane
at a white tower laced with ladders on the mountain.
"It's the mine," you mumble and I *ah*, pretending to
get it; it's my new policy. "Did you ever work there?" I ask.
"No one who ever worked there is alive to answer
that question," you say. Golden State comrade, your stone
face could save my life here. "California was beautiful—
not like this," I fret. "Nothing's ever been
like this," you never, ever fret.

Lean Seasons, Desperate Dances

What can you tell us about this object you've brought in to the show today?

Well, it was my grandfather's first anniversary gift to my grand-mother, and it's hung on the wall in their dining room for as long as I can remember.

It's a human foot.

Yes.

And this braid pattern of indentations around the ankle?

It's from the rope that hung it on the wall.

I see. What do you know about the foot?

Well, it has this mark on the heel [   ] but I couldn't find it on the internet.

That doesn't surprise me because this foot is actually your grand-father's much older foot, from the body he didn't know yet when he cut it off.

So . . . he didn't know he was cutting off his foot?

Which was fairly common. Young men cut off their future feet and gave them away as presents or ate them or used them as ashtrays. This—

Wow!

—is a nineteenth-century sock stretcher made from a past/future foot. Notice the brass studs and dovetails here and here. It's an excellent specimen.

I never saw him limping or anything.

People didn't miss their feet until their future became their present.

And that was . . . ?

At death, usually. But the details on this particular foot—like this fleck of chipped nail polish—see here?

Yeah.

And the Band-Aid around the wart on the pinkie toe?
    Ah.
These would only be found in the twentieth century, and the fresh
hacksaw marks, I'm thinking in the last half hour—

   . . .

and the blood all over the floor—
    So how much?

Two

Drones

Friends, we're living in a golden, fleeting moment
wherein rich people are buying very expensive toys
that fly higher than airplanes and can land anywhere—
on your fire escape, in your yard—and photograph you
through your curtains with a surveillance camera, record
things you're saying with a high-powered microphone.
Scientists originally built the toy to murder people
in other countries, and now rich people in this country
want to buy them. Why? I have absolutely no idea, but
I can't wait to kill one: shoot it with a shotgun, shoot it
with the hose, wing it with rocks, pick the wings off,
light it on fire, and stomp the plastic bits to splinters.
Rich people will be outraged that their toys are being
destroyed, then lobbyists will make destroying the toys
illegal, so we must move fast. The cleverest of us
already are: down in our basements, under the gun.

Certainty Is Born of Pain

Biting down wrong would've done it.
Too many chips scarfed at happy hour.
Don Cuco's two-buck margaritas, 4–6.
I've never been big on chewing. I more like
chomp-chomp-chomp-gulp. A Hoover.
Maybe I'm trying to power through the meal
to the empty place on the other side where I can
stuff more in, no subtleties of pleasure slowing
me down. A Komodo dragon unhinges its jaw
to swallow whole sick pigs and dozing deer.
Afterwards, it sleeps hours as the prey's shape
dissipates into its guts like the face on a melting coin.
I envy its contentment—or whatever you call it.
So who knows why, when I was nineteen, I got that
horribly swollen taste bud worthy of an ER visit,
but I do know when I cut it off with toenail clippers
it bled for days—hurt way worse—like my tongue
needed a cast—and now when people speak
of piercing their tongues, I know I know
too much to follow them there.

The Stendhal-Santa Syndrome

Christmas carols eviscerate me.
How the hell do people sing
"Join the triumph of the skies!"
without sobbing? I pulled
an Irish goodbye when they broke out
the tattered songbooks at the office Christmas party,
turned off the road home and bawled till I was empty.
My friend says it's the same for her when
she holds a baby. Something about
the promise of it: so fat, so happy
to make the scene—a pure manifestation
of love. This occurs to me: the listening chokes
me up, but the singing along overwhelms me.
So the tears begin in my voice
(the call is coming from inside the house!)
when, so moved by its sincerity, I'm
compelled to wade into that
clunky old body of water, open
my mouth, and drown.

The Kensington Stables

The loping *clop-clop* of the shadow ghosts' caravan parts
waves of joggers, cyclists, picnicking Dominican clans,
Hasidim, Bangladeshis. All fall silent as the horses pass
heads bowed, old sway backs unburdened by child riders
whose Down's Syndrome faces draw double takes—
effulgent sand dune faces, giddy at the sun's new nearness.
The busted beasts sleep half a block off Prospect Park
in pens mucked out by sullen teens and carny types—or so they seemed
to me whenever Sharon insisted we visit "my horse." That's what
she called the spotted one at whom she chattered like an aunt.
And it did seem to know her. Walking by alone one evening,
I saw a horse lying in the street on its side in a hose puddle
breathing heavy, surrounded by little girls gently petting it
and cooing. Imagine what it is to die like that: your killer
size immobilized and patronized by pink glittery nails
and sticky hands as if you were harmless, or a unicorn.

Ear Way in Hay the Uhnee May

The Money was hovering over us in a gelatinous spaceship
made of pink light—a jellyfishesque dry-ice carnival ride
blaring Foghat. Its uncanny feathered edges called to us,
"Pole vault into my humming-throbbing, kids!" We were
(sobbing? no, not yet) dazzled by the fish, large as cattle cars,
swimming inside it: clown fish, angelfish, electric eels . . .
"It done eht up every kind of thing and got bigger at it!"
marveled Ma, moments before she began speaking in tongues—
the briny green tongue of swine—and got beamed up into it.
This is her collection of California maps. Note how on each,
she made an X by the sea.

Hard Winter

We took it without talking about it—
every day, a new muddy bottom
to lose a barge pole to. I gave away
the pretty basket with the needles
and the magnifying glass. Let the ice
have it. Only one person at a
time sings, and the song swims up
on us like a spider bite,
beams like a coin swept
out of a corner.

But it don't buy much:
a man, a fair-
weather plan, etc.

The Women in the Woods

are outnumbered by shadows growing up and
big, like zippers, or backwards lightning over
the tight throngs of pines around them. Some are
wearing hoods. All are wearing uncomfortable
shoes that seemed comfortable in the store.
Shadows roll up and over the credit card machines
like gibberish through an emergency room intercom.
Heel spurs and hammer toes are hiding under their skin
like spring pollen in a frozen stalk. They rub their eyes
in all seasons, split open in spots, do elimination diets,
call for follow-up appointments . . . Shadows roll over
their phones getting dirty in the bottoms of their purses.
Shadows roll over the messages inside the phones.
Sometimes the message is all shadow. Sometimes it's
something good like, "Sleep in tomorrow, for
Pete's sake." Thus, Pete the Shadow is born.

The Night Drive

begins at dawn, already stressing
the next sleep so hard, getting there,
the golden day before her glazes.

By noon, a sure-fire plan
involving Benadryl, or Ambien,
or Benadryl and Ambien.

By dusk, she's stashed hills
of pills in her cheeks, economy
sized, two for the price of *timber.*

She savvies Michael Jackson's
jonesing for his strings cut (a plug
to pull) was not for death
nor any single end—it was for
seeming ends to end. Bye-bye

to nightly descension obsessions,
to cold mazes of canal locks,
to ins hiding at the back of out doors,
to the twirling double Dutch ropes
some lucky ducks jump in and sync with thoughtlessly.

I can take myself so far away,
I won't know my name
when you try to call me back.

By midnight, over pavement wearing
thin, she hauls her sled bed back into
a wood so deep she knows only its edge.

Big-Term Memory Loss

A raven swoops down upon the dawn's first
idea before she writes it down, as if it were
delectable garbage—a burrito nub or donut.
The idea's still wet, its shape yet

to emerge, but odds are it's bunk (and face it:
getting more bunk these evening days)
but she cups the meeping pinkie in her hands and
it vanishes. Fuck. So . . . onto the next one.

Where's it at? she asks the raven who has turned
into a turd in the grass and now wants
nothing from her. Jerk. Happy hoots float up
from the fairgrounds. *Damn 4-H kids*

with their giddy minds and rabbit pens. How
their laughter builds and fades and builds
behind the town's new invisible fence.

Me Time

Passed out on top of the engine
of a slow riding mower
going in a circle, circle, circle . . .

flabby sunburned arms
bounce (I'm trying
to fly!) when it hits a

dip. I've burned an unfillable
groove in the grass,
oh, you betcha.

I can see through the binoculars
that my mouth is open,
drool unfurls from it like spunk.

I know I'm snoring but cannot hear
me. All sound's been obliterated
by "Rhinestone Cowboy"

    there's been a load
    of compromisin'
    on the road to my horizon

on infinite repeat, echoing
through all the loudspeakers
hanging in the trees.

Glen Campbell as
a million Glen Campbells, as
a million-warrior army.

Good thing we live in the country.
This horseshit would never fly
(there's that word again!) in town.

You'll be home soon.
I must wake myself up and
put on some lipstick

but just on my lips
this time. Color
inside the lines.

Me Time II

A ringleted tot
traipsing through woods
on her way to
more traipsing,
masturbating, etc.

She is all that!
A new red cape
procured with
a maxed-out credit card.

    Did someone say "cape"?
    Google: cape sale

How the world has
rocked her in a cradle
all these years!

A roach observes her
from the summit of a pile of purple
pantyhose
with holes in the toes.

    "You think you're better than me?"
    ". . . Yeah."

She traipses on—
over curbs, potholes, police

tape, barricades, nails,
smoldering pits, until

a mirror
hiding in the branches
like a tiger trap.

Where are my glasses?
Oh! I am the wolf—
stooped and foiled,
huffing and puffing.

Crazy Hairdo, Crazier Head

Spector pinned down twins LaFlora and LaFauna like butterflies, trimmed their teeth, and ran them into an unlit corner of the ring on sold-out Pay-per-view. Someone said, "Hell no!" [cue laugh track] and called the cops. "Sorry my nieces are nuisances, officer." Cops gave the girls back to Spector on a platter. If you keep your silver voice down, it don't matter what's in your hand. In Phil's case, it was a suitcase, seeping, and a sawed-off shotgun cocked in broad daylight. Balls. Sirens near . . . disappear. As long as there's cash in chemo, diseases will flow like springs— water bottled, poisoned, dyed hot pink and pumped through Spector's sprinklers. "And he's a mother on the mower," says good-natured LaFlora with a wink while fetching the bastard's hash and hammer. LaFauna nods behind the blindfold, holds her breath between concrete beams in the basement.

Nazi Art

The Nazi artist wasn't really a Nazi. He simply made Nazi
art sixty years after the Holocaust as if Nazis had made it,
art about Nazis that Nazis would've loved to look at
in a Nazi museum: Nazi paintings of little idyllic towns
flooded with goose-stepping Nazis, an intricately carved
wooden Nazi hugging another intricately carved wooden Nazi,
bronze Nazi officers' caps with quotes in German praising
Nazis on the brim, everything spiraling with gold leaf swastikas.
But the Nazi artist himself was not a Nazi. *Nazi art and Nazis
were great subjects for art!* he maintained. Museums of today
loved his Nazi art because it wasn't really believed, not Nazi-felt—
it was make-believe, a commentary on Nazis. It was funny
or something, but not really. It was—er, ironically (?) Nazi.
Then people discovered the Nazi artist was an *actual* Nazi.
The museum president packed his art into a giant crate marked
NO TOUCH and stuffed it in the dark museum basement.
The curator still tiptoes past the crate remembering a time
its contents felt safe, or something; then he feels ashamed,
or something. Whatever it is, it's a real, really felt feeling.

Radical Honesty Night

"I have to give up drinking entirely or just be drunk all the time," Margie said.

"Have you ever read *The Myth of Monogamy*? Here—" Douglas handed her a copy he had apparently been sitting on all night, "—I'm having an affair and, no, I don't want to talk about it."

"My sexual fantasies are all about pony play and I don't appear in any of them."

"There's yet another excellent reason to read that book, hon," Douglas said and lit his pipe.

"Is there anything else you'd like to tell me?" Margie asked.

"Nothing that I'm aware of," Douglas said but changed his mind. "You'd think sheep when they're being sheared would thrash around, right? Turns out they just sit there like lumps, staring straight at the camera. That's what they did in the documentary I watched last night about sheep shearing."

"Last night?"

"Yeah, when I told you I was out changing the oil, I was really at a herding bar watching documentaries about sheep."

"Maybe we can work this into our sex life," Margie suggested.

"No, because when I fantasize about sheep, it's about a specific sheep named Drummond and I'm standing right next to him and he's looking me right in the eyes."

Margie shuddered. "You're right, it wouldn't work."

She pulled back the curtain and looked out of the living room window into the dark. Doug's cherry tobacco smelled like a dying sun.

"I think I'm afraid of my own success," she said.

"Duh!" Doug said, and gestured broadly.

Waiting on the Ambulance

This music feels like a paper cut the size of my face, on my face.
Normally, I find the song very relaxing—there's only two notes,
and the singer's talking about a cowboy. The way it just kind of
rocks back and forth like a teeter-totter. I was going to say
something about fat people on the teeter-totter but then I thought,
"You could stand to lose a pound or two yourself, kiddo." So it's
just a teeter-totter with nobody on it. This kind of questioning—
fretting over the feelings of imaginary fat people—may very well
be what's making me tired. I've had a long day, I think.
Did you ever see that *Twilight Zone* where a woman
named Barbara walks into a department store and she's really a
mannequin on shore leave living as a real person for one month
but she forgets who she is? The other mannequins are waiting for
her to return so they can take a turn being real. When the mannequin
manager reminds her who she is, Barbara's not mad at all. "Oh,
of course. I remember now. I'm not real." And she apologizes for
making them wait. I thought that showed a lot of class on her part.
I feel I'm waiting on a message like that: someone's about to tell me
something and everything will fall into place, make a heck of a lot
more sense. This is a lovely home you have here. I have a what?
Where? On my face? Here? Here? Here? Here? Here?

The Body Is Its Own Thermometer

Having lost all faith in my own memory,
I was taking notes in the doctor's office.
"First, you'll lose the ability to write,"
he said, as my hand suddenly cramped up
and drove the pen off the paper. I wondered
what he would possibly say next. "Then
you'll begin to wonder a lot . . . mostly about
possibilities . . ." That's weird, I thought.
". . . and how weird things are . . ." My heart
began to pound—I felt dizzy. ". . . accelerated
pulse, lightheadedness . . ." "Stop," I said,
closing my eyes. "Your eyes will close, panic
will set in—and you know what the biggest killer
in the forest is?" "You?" I gasped.
"You wish!" he hawed.

"It's Hard to Shtup a Snake, But Not Impossible!"

The audience thought the song sucked eggs and so did the sponsors—especially the soap guys. "Get that douchebag off the stage," I saw one say—read his lips through the sound booth windows. It's the same old story: pigs before swine. If I was a beauty queen, I'd be Miss Understood. Ha ha.

So I asked Sam (because I do care): "Was it the farts, the fake mustache, or the Nazi costume?"

He made a face like he wasn't just at the end of his rope, he was long past it and living in Connecticut with a wife and kids I'd never met and he meant to keep it that way. A don't-go-out-in-the-garage-with-Uncle-Marty-alone kind of thing. I'd seen him shoot that face at yo-yos for years but not at me. Sam had blown a special bubble around me made of plastic or satin not water, so if it popped I wouldn't get wet. But apparently, the bubble'd gone the way of the dodo.

Sam passed on the wrap-up drinks. I didn't. When I got back to the apartment, my twin was wide awake, coloring pictures in front of the TV.

"What's that, sweetie?" I pointed to the red line, arching over a circle and sticks I recognized as me. The rest of the rainbow was coming, maybe? Hopefully?

"Eeeengh," she moaned like a moose.

She drew another body on its side, under my legs. And another. And another. Then long drops of blue rain falling on it all. Both a moon and sun hung in the sky. Above the green ground line: flowers. Below: a devil in his hell.

Impulsive Grooming Syndrome

I thought I was doing a pretty good job back there
cutting my own hair. In the moment, it felt right
enough to dis the ultimate mirror as mirage—oily
pores crowned with bald patches—slack, gawky kook
stuck in Fluff. "Who is that?" "You." "Yeah, right."
Right enough in the nipple-hard moment—electric,
singular static. Doubtless, any kid with an ID card
would know the right-enough it felt was not enough.
I had to lose an ear before I figured it out. Oh moment,
how you blow me. I've given you my whole foggy
life, and now my stereo. Bitte, reveal if what passes
for enough these days, is? This breed's life expectancy is ____.

Shells

Abandoned in the grooved
seat cushion of your armchair
on a red Fiestaware plate:

a pile of sunflower seeds,
dusty as elephants, fruit still
locked in their gray shells.

Beside them, a neat hill of shards
like beetle wings: sucked clean
and cracked like a champ.

We move the plate into the kitchen,
cover it in plastic wrap in hopes
you'll be home soon. At our feet,
little dogs worry and whine.

The Only Man in Grandma Land Grows to Love
His Hand-Knit Mittens More

Think *ginger*

or *cream horns*—

Norway

in slowmo

on a motorless boat

born

for dry dock

suspended

like a taxidermied goose

you see up the skirt of—

or bawdy sailors'

yo-ho-hos

echoing eons

like a whale's song:

Yorrrrhoooohoooo . . .

Our work

is endless.

Full stop.

You heard me.

Endless.

Celery

and *sour milk.*

Don't think

sprinkles.

That frilly pink

                              time's poured

out,

     little teapot,

                    like your ever-blurring

blue tattoos.

Auld Lang Syne

Dad couldn't stop crying after Kathy moved him into the facility. When she came to visit, he'd cry and say he wanted to die. He said the same thing to the nurses. This went on for about a month until the doctor put him on an antidepressant especially for Parkinson's patients. The next time Kathy came to visit, she found him in the cafeteria, talking to some of the other residents and not crying at all—just enjoying his lunch. When it was time for her to go, he didn't cry, but rather calmly escorted her to the car. "Do you like this car? My wife and I were thinking about getting one," he told her. "That's very interesting," Kathy smiled, "because I *am* your wife." Dad chuckled, "Is that right?" He squinted over the palm trees towards the freeway. So many cars. Busy busy busy. "Well, we'll see you later, then," he said, and shook her hand firmly, the way he'd learned to do at Rotary. What funny new friends he was making.

Three

A Fairy Tale

When my father was nine years old, his mother said, "Tommy, I'm taking you to the circus for your birthday. Just you and me. And I'll buy you anything you want." The middle child of six, my father thought this was the most incredible, wonderful thing that had ever happened to him—like something out of a fairy tale.

They got in the car, but instead of driving him to the circus, his mother pulled up in front of the hospital and told him to go inside and ask for Dr. So-and-so. After that, they'd go to the circus.

So he went inside and asked for Dr. So-and-so. A nurse told him to follow her into a room where she closed the door and gave him a shot. My father fell asleep, and some hours later, woke up crying in agony with his tonsils gone. A different nurse got him dressed and sent him outside where his mother was waiting in the car with the engine running. He couldn't speak on the way home to ask her, "What about the circus?" Days later, when he could, he didn't. They never mentioned it again.

Fifty-eight years later, he tells this story to his wife, his only explanation, when she asks him, "What are you doing home from church so early?"

He'd walked out in the middle of "A Mighty Fortress Is Our God," never to return.

The Real River

"The real river flows under the river."

—James Galvin

Gauze gaze, the present's freeze never sticks.
Its microbes twitch in the ice like fat ticks.
Its frames orbit a light source we can't see offscreen,
only its reflection-slash-refraction buried deep
in dark glass throws its lariat of luminescence
'round the shade cows coming home from a hard
day ambling. Stars sit stiller than herds, but still swim
lifetimes to be regarded by us—how flattering!—
we, stuck like gum on smog's shoe and true-bling blind.
Where's the stars' ticker-tape parade? The Kiwanis's
wooden welcome sign swinging at our city's edge?
How many Avon ladies' *ding-dongs* go unopened—
Skin So Soft sloshing in their kits like penicillin?
Or are they already over like the frog and songbird?
If not yet, soon enough, for sure: future starlight e'er
blows o'er their thinning hairlines, the pink marrow
of their effortful atoms bleeds out like sugar in snow.
Do pancake stacks of hope, seven-layer dips of evil
mourn some or sum of history's smushedness?
Who cares. See grass left behind in the fissure,
writhing white lichen, and walls you pop through
like how Bugs punked Daffy in "Duck Amuck."
"Look on my works, ye Mighty, and despair!"
tantrumed the tyrant, but see how easily his bloat
shuttered, how all tyrants' dresses get pressed at last
like pansies between a Bible's yellowing pages. It's
cool what flashes endure, how blood bubbles blue
beneath the black-and-white curtain. Romans led
animals from conquered lands into the Colosseum—

peacocks, elephants, gorillas—and tore them apart,
only to see what their deaths resembled, hear their
endgame. Light blew through their hides, then
through the hands that held their leashes.
Wonder of the World, my eye. Crumble away, creeps.
Your walls fold like origami in the innermost matryoshka.
Flavius, shmavius. Here's your parade, stars,
your homecoming float, your flitsy
tissue-paper monoliths.
At first sight: stone.
At second: foam.

Hive Mind

Riding in the car with my mother, I never graduated from the backseat to the front. Whenever I tried to climbing in next to her ("This is stupid—I'm riding up front"), she'd howl and swipe at me until I caved. That was how she defended her space. We drove around like that until I got my driver's license: us two, locked in the dust-mote mottled skies of our own minds, counting things. Me: syllables and the shadows of telephone poles falling across the car. Her: I don't know. She can't describe her OCD to me— only that it has to do with numbers—some inexplicable tally she's been running all her life. I imagine it like a spider's web, easily disturbed, then dispersed by the breath of other people. Whatever its shape, it's the only thing that's ever soothed her.

One stalk of corn can't bear fruit by itself. It needs other stalks around to pollinate. Even a single row won't cut it. The Mandan knew to grow them in circles, my boyfriend tells me. And sunflowers, his father adds, grown in a row will take turns bending north, then south, etc., down the line to give each other a shot at the light. We're in the garden after dinner. Suddenly I envy anything that moves itself to accommodate another: a subtle shift to the left or right, self-preservation that could pass for love.

All the Other Lights

The hawk perched on the hand of a Christ-
on-the-cross-shaped stoplight pole's a scoping
ring—feathers pale as the prairie it's married.
Earth falls in all ways away from it. No thing's
invisible: tinkle sprinkled around a burrow's
buried door: ultra-ultraviolet. Mouseketeers
with peeps too low for stethoscopes are loud
as screeching brakes in the traffic under its feet.
The speed cars go is not really time in its eyes.
It knows, or learned, that's fake—some unseen
joker loop-de-looping a laser-pointer dot.
We're blind to all the other lights winking away
out there. A gray rabbit loping over dirty snow
eclipses aurorae at both poles and rainbows.

Babies & Bagpipes

Stooped by bulging backpacks, we plodded along
waterlogged plywood set atop the flood and mud
that dried like whitewash on our pink feet once we'd
shed our soaked expensive sandals, and settled in
a spot on deck, under the roof, out of the tyrannical
equatorial sun. Miles below, the invisible Wallace Line
marked where the sea floor fell away. Trees grew
scrubbier on islands we puttered past.
A Jackie Chan movie was playing on the snack bar TV.
The polite Indonesians kept their eyes on the set.
Doubtless, we reeked worse than animals to them:
our sweat born of idleness, ice cream, and beer.
Onscreen, in a funeral scene for an Irish cop, bagpipes
woke and groaned to life, and babies held in the arms
of the people around us—in carriages and bassinets,
swaddled in pristine white blankets—began to cry
in unison, same note as the pipes, same prehistoric,
birdlike moaning *heeennhh*. We adults all met
eyes, raised our brows, chuckled, shrugged,
and agreed without words: *This is weird—this song
all of us know, but none of us remember.*

The Killer

Stella had been chasing that rabbit for weeks.
While wet nose deep in the lilies, she'd miss
its streak across the lawn, its slip into a skinny
woodpile nook just wide enough to scotch
a frantic paw. She must've thought the flickering
thing magic. "It darts into the bush and disappears!"
And so all the more other to her—its white tail, a
wink, a "so long, dummy!"—its siren otherness
setting her fur on end like lightning. Tirelessly
she worked the corners, fluffed the undergrowth,
until finally she laid down with that flash, draped
one leg across the broken back and licked it
head to toe, tasting all it still was, its open black
eye steering towards some other she'd erased.

Yellow Rose

She'd done it once before, last fall:
stood on one foot—the other drawn
up like a clenched fist.

She was that way a week: dragging
the bad half of her tapered body up and
down the cage bars like a heavy sled.

Female parakeets, the vet said, have one ovary
on the left leg. When inflamed, it can paralyze
the whole left side. It doesn't hurt—it's numb.

She got a shot and was fast back to two legs.
So when it happened again, this time on the
right, I told the new vet, "Just give her that shot."

He showed me, among her yellow feathers,
where to feel for the tumor, big as a marble
at the top of her skinny pink leg.

What were the odds? Paralyzed twice in one life.
The first time: simply solved. The next: not.

"She's from Texas," he said, smiling at her.
He'd looked up the number on her ankle band.

And there we are: in the hands of strangers, still
discovering basic things about ourselves, like
where we came from, right up to the end.

The Mushroom Burial Suit

Screwed onto a silky stem with one arm
Buried to the elbow in a skirt of breathy gills,
A smooth hill of snow caps trace the nose
(Once sneezing), shoulders (once shuddering)
And paunch (once hanging over a waistband).
Busy bees, spores fly below the eye's radar
To lay and lay down their carpet—soon, seamless
As fondant, they'll break down the splitting
Skin, blood, bones, and acorns sprouting in the now
Vacant mouth, down through a life of fretting
And flurry to the ground thriving under.

Annie's Song

Of course his renditions of "Love on the Rocks," "Big Bad John," and "Suspicious Minds" were top-drawer. What would you expect from a 300-pound karaoke DJ bear wearing a flannel shirt and elastic-waist jeans? But when his baritone boom lifted like a let-go balloon into "Annie's Song," I was so surprised, I cried. It had been another very long day—another day I hadn't downloaded QuickBooks, another day I'd skipped my posture exercises.

I'd performed a balance beam routine to it in junior high school. The other girls had all picked harder songs like "My Sharona" and "We Will Rock You." I thought choosing John Denver meant I was different—more genteel. And I was different: I looked like the fat kid in Bad Santa, and they looked like porn stars. I must've looked especially dumb in my sagging white tube socks: mouth open, looking down the entire time but still about to fall.

Later that night, the karaoke DJ and I did a shot of Fireball together. "I've never drunk Fireball before," I said. "Oh, you'll like it," he assured me, "it's very popular."

I dreamed I moved to a cabin in the woods with no electricity. As a poet, it was the only environmentally responsible thing to do even though, I knew, I would have to kill myself when I got too old to work. "What a bummer," I thought and suddenly I was wrapping my mouth around a shotgun barrel so real, I could taste it—like pencil lead. "How is that possible?" I wondered, then my friend, M, dream-texted me:

"Help! Trapped at a remote finishing school! Come get me!"

"They still have finishing schools?" I texted back.

"Questionable ideas have answers, too," she replied.

Poem for Thelma Ritter

Cue eye roll. Housecoat sleeves shrug-flutter
like signal flags to the ship: "Give it a rest, saps."
Pocketbook handy lighter quick-flick snap that's that.
Worn brown shoe heel like a sturdy ass on a barstool.
Seams: sorta straight. Sewn into an old broad's suit
again (don't start with the ladies in Wardrobe—
they're union) though her cheeks are full and eyes
unlined (especially next to crepey Bette). Ruffles bubble
out the neck of her party dress like five o'clock beer foam.
Home-late headlights sizing up a sink full of dishes.
I must've lost track of time. Wives should always be
lovers, too. Fake thin-lipped grin. Like a sheep herder
watching the blonde run away in tears, across the road
was the last time I saw her, officer. Don't tell no one
I told you: [whispers] I'm the ringer in the jingle contest.

Caring for Your New Perm

I started to write a poem about
giving a dog a perm. It was really
about how the need to control people
is as absurd as forcing an animal to be
something other than it is: putting tiny
high heels on a bird, etc. The dog wanted
dreadlocks so the speaker—a "we"—
shaved its head. That's where I stopped.
"I'm afraid for that dog," I thought
on my way down to the basement
to load the wet laundry in the dryer.
Suddenly, I wanted to tell you how much
I love you, to apologize for the notes
stuck to your bathroom mirror, the frantic
green exclamation points. I was afraid for
you like I was that dog. Upstairs, I erased
the lines and listened to the laundry spin—
heating up. Why, oh, why won't
you listen to me?

"Schenectady Is Most Definitely

a hyperbolic landscape full of empty swimming pools,
violent men with tight asses straining the seams of their acid-
washed jeans, pizza swamps of molten cheese with slices,
like my heart, *rrrrrripped out*—like starfish missing arms,
but opposite—inverted—or something," my voice trails
off but my hands keep miming a triangle shape in the air,
tepeeing it pointy and knifey to show him the purport of that
invisible missing piece, its edge so etched in my brain. Then
one hand slips down the other side like a bathtub spider so
I climb back up the spout . . .

                       "Did you take your crazy pills?"
he asks. "I don't have anything to swallow them with," I reply,
about to cry. He pulls over, we get out, I follow him into
the branches of an overgrown cloud of a hedge, green
as animal eyes, to a blue pool hidden in the middle.
"Swallow them with that," he points at the water.
"It's full of chemicals," I insist. "Not for years,"
he grins. I bend down to the water, "You're like
an almanac—*gulp gulp.*" Somehow, again, I'd
missed the shy emptying and filling,
the husk, bud and bloom.

The Decorative Airport Fern Is Not What It Pretends to Be

and it takes me a triple take to realize it's scanning
me, or something near my ear—that must be it. No plant's
ever complimented my perfume—wait—there it goes
again. Did you see that? [Time passes, drinks] "Sure, I
remember when I thought you were a fern but you were!
Who could blame me?" I tell the what's now a magnificent
purple tetrahedron, with mighty dicks all over its corners, just
a hint of ferniness remains in its fingertips—enough to blush.
We hug goodbye. The smell of flowers lingers around me
the next day. Flying home, a decorative airport fern that really
is a decorative airport fern says, "You smell nice." I don't
believe it, but it's still a happy
ending.

Cue: *Action Man* Theme

Who's gonna wake and bake
and clean the bottom of the lake
and shovel all of the snow
from the yard?
It's so hard
to do so
with the snow
when it's a hundred and thirty below!

Action man!
He's a man of action!
Action man!
He's so hypervigilant!

Who's driving with a beer between his knees,
and sweeping all the dog hair in a pile,
and wiping off countertops?
He don't need a mop
or a doc who asks him
personal questions!

Action man!
He's a man of action!
Action man!
Here's his reading glasses!

Who's on it like vomit
and washes the germs off his hands?
Who's the man who vacuums the vacuum?
Action man!

Ladies' Night/Feeling Right

I was walking across a hotel lobby when I saw Tim, my ex, sitting with his mother and Gary near a fireplace in the bar. Tim and Gary had their heads bowed.

"What's happening?" I asked Tim's mom.

"Well, I was just telling the boys how I know Tim is gay."

Tim raised just his eyes, then lowered them again.

"How do you know?" I asked, even though I knew, too.

"Because I gave them two pairs of my underwear to take on vacation and they peed on both of them," Tim's mom said. Tim shifted a bit, but Gary looked positively elated.

"I'll tell you how *I* know Tim is gay," I said.

"How?" she asked. Her genuine interest made me feel good about what I knew.

"Because he doesn't eat pussy! *That's* why!" I said, and as Tim's face slid down his chin, all the people at the bar and behind the desk began to clap and cheer, and I pivoted on my heel and marched out through the double glass doors where my unicorn was waiting and she was like, "How'd that feel?" and I was like, "Amazing!"

9. Description of Fellowship Activities: Complete in the Space Provided. Do Not Continue on Additional Pages.

The money will be used to purchase a used school bus so I can travel with a band from community to community teaching poetry to the underserved through music, art, and interpretive dance. Each workshop will end with the beautification of a certain underserved area in the community (such as a crack house, or trash-covered vacant lot) followed by a poetry reading given by illiterate members of the community—especially young children, because poetry can not only help this population read, it can show them how to feel about reading, themselves, the community, and reading in and about the community itself. For it is in illiteracy that we find the poetry of tomorrow—and in tomorrow we find the illiterate of today. Do you have direct deposit? Do you have direct deposit? Do you have direct deposit? Do you have direct deposit? Do you have direct deposit? Do you have direct deposit? (continued on additional pages—see attached)

Henry Mancini: Now *There* Was an Entertainer

I dislike thinking things through. It itches.

I also dislike books wherein the characters take note of and can articulate everything they're thinking or have ever thought.

A Visit from the Goon Squad was like that: a woman remembering everything she was thinking about a man when she was taking a bath eight years ago.

I think our brains are just making up what we're thinking like a big stream-of-consciousness lie. A fire-hose lie with a broken nozzle.

"Oh yeah. *That's* what I thought. On purpose."

I hate snotty people and unfunny people. Their brains move so slow. It's exhausting.

Unfunny people love to think they think things on purpose—and that their thoughts are precious. Some poets think their feelings are more special than regular people.

If anything, we're handicapped by them. It's like we're a book and every word in it's highlighted. In hot pink.

"What are we supposed to do with all these pages of hot pink feelings?!"

"Throw them away."

"Are you nuts?!"

But you have to get it together. You have no choice or you would've quit this a long time ago. Lie, but not too much. Know you're lying. Lies are art! Our own names are but wind through their shadows.

Our Robots

Hal, the robot in *2001*, wants to kill the astronaut.
Forty years later, Gerty, the robot in the movie *Moon*,
wants to save the astronaut. Was *Moon* written by
a robot? No. Maybe Gerty is a nicer robot because
we're getting smarter about robots, smarter without
knowing it. That's how people get smarter: dumbly,
without knowing it, until years after the smart's set in
and we're dumb in whole new ways. It's exciting,
the ways in which we're newly dumb! Robots are
novelties. Without novelties, we'd pull our feathers out.
When the movie robot was invented, we couldn't pull
ourselves away. Some starved in the seats. We died
in front of the TV robot watching quiz-show robots,
died bowed down before the warm radio robot with its
shell-shocked boogie-woogie, died guzzling the dark
dank developing bath of the photograph robot, died
weeping with the lute robot, died screwing around
like punks with gunpowder robots, died carving stars
in stone with chisel robots, wheel robots, fire robots.
Maybe Gerty is a nicer robot because we are nicer
now (too late?) and robots have our faces. How they
follow us like baby ducks, guessing our next robot.
Ancient cave-painting robots with our faces. This one
of a buffalo hunt: there we are.

Sakura Matsuri

Bleached police ghosts come about day three
if you're one of those *Can't complain!* SOBs.
Day one for the restless rest of us, gnashing
and kicking ourselves to sleep. Jesus just makes
us sadder. And watching you bust your hump
loving Jesus? Jesus. He took one for the team
but his bearded handlers were bad mofos.
The trees are blooming furiously, Incredible-
Hulk style, blossoms swan diving into the abyss.
We should be blissed out on a tropical island
eating fake fish shaped like a party steak.
After a long night bowing deeply in dreams,
a thought: "I'm good at this!" The song
playing in the dream head: "The Blood Done
Signed My Name." So don't let 'em fool ya:
unemployment's hard work. You gotta stay
occupied. Shadowboxing, pushups. Everything
is a prison of the mind, a drawer crammed
ajar with infinite unmatched ankle socks.

Immutable

Not the ink nor the name
it sculpts in waves and slashes.
Not the clammy hands nor rash
on the ring finger nor the missing
tip, the stump, the hole where a
nose used to be—though it shocks
to hear words echoing in the skull,
to see the skull can be seen into.
Not what side of the war we died on or
under. Not the color. Not the *O*s
on each side of the *I* nor their holler.
Not the way we'll slip out of this world,
our swan songs clogging the ears of all
the wordless species going first—
"After you." They do not define us:
these skins, these sky-high
piles of hides.

Acknowledgments

Thank you to the power of infinity: Collin Switzer, Ada Limón, Deb & Denny Switzer, Shannatastic, Barbara Ching, Sarah Manguso, Meg Johnson, and LBNL Jody Knox.

Thanks to the editors of the publications in which versions of these poems first appeared.

1913   The Women in the Woods

The Ampersand Review   Ballet on the Radio; Drones; The Night Drive; The Comeback

The Awl   Certainty Is Born of Pain

B O D Y   Big Term Memory Loss; Blind Date

Boston Review   I Cast the Shadow of a Sword over Sky & Sea; Iowa Plates.

Burnside Review   Ladies Night/Feelin' Right; It's Hard to Shtup a Snake But Not Impossible!; Yellow Rose

Coldfront   I Led the Horse to Water

Conduit   Immutable; The Stendhal-Santa Syndrome

Damfino   Henry Mancini: Now *There* Was An Entertainer; Shells

The Equalizer   Cue: *Action Man* Theme

Everyday Genius   The Body Is Its Own Thermometer

Fence   Nazi Art

Gulf Coast   Between Menus

Lemon Hound   Poetry Reading at the Fried Chicken & Waffle Hut; Hard Winter; Impulsive Grooming Syndrome

Luna Luna   Hive Mind; The New *Twilight Zone*: Empty City; Schenectady Is Most Definitely

Ploughshares   Babies & Bagpipes

Plume   Our Robots; The Only Man in Grandma Land Learns to Love His Hand-Knit Mittens More; The Real River; Crazy

Hairdo, Crazier Head

Poem-a-Day for the Academy of American Poets   A Fairy
  Tale; Auld Lang Syne; The Decorative Airport Fern Is Not
  What It Pretends to Be

The Poetry Review   Sakura Matsuri

Queen Mob's Teahouse   9. Description of Fellowship
  Activities; Life's Work

The Rusty Toque   The Kensington Stables; All the Other
  Lights; Caring for Your New Perm

Southern California Review   Radical Honesty Night

Typo   Ear Way in Hay the Uhnee May

The Plot for Villainess Press   Me Time II; Poem for Thelma
  Ritter

West Wind Review   Lean Seasons, Desperate Dances;
  Waiting on the Ambulance

WSQ: Women's Studies Quarterly   Annie's Song; Me Time

About the Author

Photo credit: Alexa Vachon

Jennifer L. Knox is an iconic American poet whose work has been compared to Richard Pryor, Sarah Silverman, cartoonist R. Crumb, musician Randy Newman, and magician Doug Henning. None of these comparisons is quite right, however. Knox's work is unmistakably her own: surprisingly empathetic, utterly original, both funny and frightening, like America itself. And like the best comedians, she is never merely funny: each of her speakers has something important to say. Knox's poems have appeared four times in the *Best American Poetry* series and in the anthologies *Great American Prose Poems: From Poe to Present* and *Best American Erotic Poems*, as well as in such publications as the *New York Times*, the *New Yorker*, *American Poetry Review*, and *McSweeney's*. Her first three books of poems are also available from Bloof Books: *The Mystery of the Hidden Driveway*, *Drunk by Noon*, and *A Gringo Like Me*.

CPSIA information can be obtained at www.ICGtesting.com
Printed in the USA
LVOW10s0845201115

PP10251300002B/5/P